Witness to History

Civil Rights

Brendan January

Heinemann Library
Chicago, Illinois

Designed by Heinemann Library
Produced for Heinemann by Discovery Books Ltd
Originated by Ambassador Litho Ltd
Printed and bound in China
by South China Printing

07 06 05 04 03
10 9 8 7 6 5 4 3 2 1

**Library of Congress Cataloging-in-Publication
Data**

January, Brendan, 1972-
  Civil rights / Brendan January.
    p. cm. -- (Witness to history)
Summary: Presents a study of the civil rights
movement in the United
States.
Includes bibliographical references and index.
  ISBN 1-4034-4566-4 -- ISBN 1-4034-4574-5 (pbk.)
  1. African Americans--Civil rights--History--20th
century--Juvenile
literature. 2. Civil rights movements--United States-
-History--20th
century--Juvenile literature. 3. United States--Race
relations--Juvenile literature. [1. African Americans--
Civil
rights--History--20th century. 2. Civil rights
movements. 3. Race
relations.] I. Title. II. Witness to history (Heinemann
Library (Firm))

  E185.61.J36 2003
  323'.0973--dc21

                                2003007107

Acknowledgments
The author and publishers are grateful to the
following for permission to reproduce copyright
material:

pp. 4, 5, 13, 19, 21, 23, 24, 25, 26, 28, 29, 31, 32, 34, 36,
40, 41, 42, 43, 43, 44 Bettmann/Corbis; pp. 6, 8, 9, 11,
14, 33, 45 Peter Newark's Historical Pictures; pp. 10,
15, 16, 38 Corbis; p. 30 Corbis/Flip Schulk; p. 46
Popperfoto/Reuters; p. 48 Corbis/Ariel Skelley; p. 50
Corbis Sygma/Rubin Steven.

Cover photograph shows civil rights protesters
taking part in the March on Washington in 1963.
Reproduced with permission of Corbis.

The publishers would like to thank Bob Rees,
historian and teacher, for his assistance in the
preparation of this book.

Disclaimer
All Internet addresses (URLs) given in this book
were valid at the time of going to press. However,
due to the dynamic nature of the Internet, some
addresses may have changed, or sites may have
changed or ceased to exist since publication. While
the author and publisher regret any inconvenience
this may cause readers, no responsibility for any
such changes can be accepted by either the author
or the publisher.

Every effort has been made to contact copyright
holders of any material reproduced in this book. Any
omissions will be rectified in subsequent printings if
notice is given to the publishers.

Some words are shown in
bold, **like this.** You can find
out what they mean by looking
in the glossary.

Contents

Introduction

In the 1950s, African Americans and their supporters began an epic struggle to win **equality** in the United States. They demanded the freedoms most white Americans took for granted, such as the right to vote and the right to the protection of the law. African Americans wanted the same opportunities as whites, an equal chance of getting good jobs, nice homes, and quality schools for their children. They fought to be treated as equals to the white majority.

Through marches and **rallies,** in the courts and on the streets, African Americans broke down a system of laws and attitudes that had largely confined them to a restricted position in American society. That struggle is called the Civil Rights movement.

A nonviolent protest

The Civil Rights movement was marked by extraordinary bravery and was guided mostly by the ideas of **nonviolence** and **civil disobedience.** Demonstrators marched in groups of a few or in groups of hundreds of thousands. They made speeches and sang songs that cried out for freedom. They disobeyed laws that were unfair or that took away their rights. One of the movement's most important leaders, Martin Luther King Jr., urged his followers not to fight back if they were hit, cursed at, or attacked. Violence, he said, would only lead to more pain and bloodshed.

In the 1950s, many African Americans still struggled in a state of extreme poverty with little access to schooling, medical care, or the protection of the law. In 1958, this family of **migrant workers** lived in a small, one-room wooden shack in Virginia while they worked temporarily on a farm. After the harvest, they would move on to find more work.

In 1965, Martin Luther King Jr. led a 54-mile (86-kilometer) march from Selma to Montgomery, Alabama, where he demanded that Governor George Wallace stop police brutality and help African Americans exercise their right to vote.

King's words were important because the Civil Rights movement was bitterly resisted. For hundreds of years, white Americans had enjoyed more rights than African Americans. Sadly, many whites still believed they were superior to African Americans and did not want change. But even though on one occasion firefighters were ordered to turn their powerful water hoses on crowds of African-American marchers and police unleashed snarling attack dogs, the protests could not be stopped.

Changing attitudes

The civil-rights demonstrators carried on their protests even when they faced angry white mobs. Demonstrations continued after many civil rights leaders were killed and after Martin Luther King Jr., the leading voice in the Civil Rights movement, was **assassinated**. In the end, the movement led to the introduction of new laws that protected African Americans' rights. More importantly, many people embraced new attitudes about what it meant to be white, black, and American. By the end of the 1960s, the United States had been changed forever.

How Do We Know?

Historians examine primary sources—documents, recordings, or objects—to reconstruct and learn about the past. For example, newspapers are primary sources. They provide accounts of events as they occurred. Letters and diaries reveal how people felt and thought as history unfolded around them. Speeches are more formal and provide a record of how leaders publicly tried to create change. Photographs provide images of figures and scenes. In more recent times, film footage has captured historical events as they happened, such as President John F. Kennedy's **assassination** in 1963 or the terrorist attack on the World Trade Center in September 2001.

The power of primary sources

The Civil Rights movement developed at a time when television was becoming popular and more common. For the first time, millions of people could see moving images of an event almost as it occurred. What they saw would determine how the nation's leaders reacted to events, especially the Civil Rights movement. These images are also valuable historical **artifacts** that are carefully studied today.

Historians also seek out stories and accounts given by people who were involved in movements and events of the time. These accounts, called oral histories, give a very personal and intimate view of the Civil Rights movement.

Getting to the truth

Primary sources can be biased or inaccurate. Some sources are created quickly, just after an event. People forget or confuse facts and they misspell names. They may make mistakes or just not remember properly. Sometimes people have prejudices or opinions that may influence the way they report an event. If someone dislikes the government, for example, he or she is less likely to give an **unbiased** account of that government's activities. It is the historian's job to carefully read through the sources and determine what is most accurate. Historians can compare sources to judge what actually occurred. To research the Civil Rights movement, historians also look to **secondary sources.** These are sources that come to the historian secondhand. They are often accounts written long after the events took place. Historians, today and in the future, will use primary and secondary sources to tell the story of the Civil Rights movement. This is how they write the history that appears in books, textbooks, and magazines. They will use the sources to write descriptions, narrate events, and answer important questions, such as what was life in the United States like before the movement, what happened during the movement, and what have we become since?

Televisions became a common item in American households during the 1950s and 1960s. Through television the entire nation saw firsthand the images of interracial violence, protests, and speeches from national leaders. In this picture, President John F. Kennedy is giving a speech.

Slavery

The first Africans to live in North America were taken from Africa against their will. They were unloaded in chains in Jamestown, Virginia, in 1619, only a decade after a group of English people founded a colony there. The colonists desperately needed workers to clear thick forests and plant crops, such as tobacco.

Slavery has existed in different forms throughout history in countries such as Great Britain, China, Italy, Egypt, and Russia. In some cultures, enslaved people were allowed to earn their freedom or could keep their children from being enslaved. In the Americas, however, slavery evolved into a particularly brutal form. Slavery became associated with dark skin color, and children of slaves were kept in **bondage.**

By the early 1800s, slavery had spread throughout the United States. Most enslaved people lived in the South. Africans were loaded onto boats—mainly from the West African countries of Angola, Nigeria, the Ivory Coast, and Sierra Leone—and taken across the Atlantic Ocean to ports in the South. There, the slaves were taken from the ships and sold in large markets. Slaves performed all kinds of tasks, from toiling in cotton fields to cooking in **plantation** mansions. They had no rights. It was illegal for whites to teach them to read or write. Slaves were treated as property, like horses. Punishment for disobedience could range from a light whipping to death.

This picture shows a slave market in Virginia during the 1850s. This African family, after having been taken by force from their home country, then had to face the devastation of being sold at a slave market.

Olaudah Equiano's account

Olaudah Equiano was born in 1745 in what is now the country of Nigeria. He was sold into slavery when he was eleven years old. Eventually, he bought his freedom and moved to England. Equiano was one of few slaves able to write about his life as a slave. In 1789, he published *The Interesting Narrative of the Life of Olaudah Equiano, or Gustavus Vassa, Written by Himself*. In the passage below, he describes his experience boarding a slave ship.

The first object which saluted my eyes when I arrived on the coast was the sea, and a slave ship, which was then riding at anchor, and waiting for its cargo. These filled me with astonishment, which was soon converted into terror. When I was carried on board, I was immediately handled, and tossed up, to see if I were sound [healthy], by some of the crew, and I was now persuaded that I had gotten into a world of bad spirits and that they were going to kill me. Their complexions too differing so much from ours, their long hair, and the language they spoke which was very different from any I had ever heard united me to [convinced me of] this belief.

Olaudah Equiano is painted here wearing the clothes of an English gentleman.

Resistance and Rebellion

By the mid-1800s, about 4 million slaves lived in the United States, mostly in the South. In the houses of the cities and among the rows of slave shacks on **plantations,** slaves resisted their **bondage.**

Many slaves decided to seize freedom by escaping to the northern states, where slavery had been outlawed by 1860. Some free blacks and northern whites helped slaves escape north by establishing what was called the underground railroad. The railroad was actually a series of safe hiding places, where escaping slaves could spend the night before resuming their journey north.

Freed slaves faced severe **discrimination** in the northern states as well, but they could move about freely. Some of them held meetings and began publishing newspapers and holding **rallies** demanding the **abolition** of slavery.

Other resistance to slavery was more violent. On August 21, 1831, in Southampton County, Virginia, a slave named Nat Turner and a group of other slaves seized weapons and began attacking white households. By the time Turner and his 75 followers were killed or captured, 60 white people had been killed. The **rebellion** shook the white South to its core. Before Nat Turner, many white southerners had believed slaves were simple people who were content, even happy, with their situation. Turner showed this belief to be entirely false.

Henry Bibb's letter
Henry Bibb escaped slavery and fled to Detroit, Michigan. He wrote this letter to his former master in 1844.

Frederick Douglass, an escaped slave, wrote a masterful narrative about his experiences and led the fight against slavery through his newspaper, the *North Star.* The paper was named after the star escaped slaves used to guide themselves northward to freedom.

Many slaves tried to escape their miserable situation. Plantation owners regularly placed advertisements in the newspaper that described the features and character of the slave, along with a reward for his or her return.

I thank God that I am not property now, but am regarded as a man like yourself, and although I live far north, I am enjoying a comfortable living by my own industry. If you should ever chance to be traveling this way, and will call on me, I will use you better than you did me while you held me as a slave. Think not that I have any malice [ill will] against you, for the cruel treatment which you inflicted on me while I was in your power. As it was the custom of your country, to treat your fellow men as you did me and my little family, I can freely forgive you.

You may perhaps think hard of us for running away from slavery, but as to myself, I have but one apology to make for it, which is this: I have only to regret that I did not start at an earlier period. I might have been free long before I was.

Civil War and Reconstruction

The issue of slavery bitterly divided the northern and southern states. Free blacks in the North, and many whites as well, saw slavery as a brutal and savage system. Southern whites angrily defended it as their way of life. Equally important was the fact that the entire economy of the South depended on slavery. Slaves worked the **plantations,** the mines, and all manufacturing industries. When Abraham Lincoln was elected president in 1860, he promised to **abolish** slavery. The southern states decided to **secede** and the nation disintegrated into bloody **civil war.**

About 180,000 African Americans served in the **Union** army and navy during the Civil War, which lasted from 1861 to 1865. In January 1863, the Emancipation Proclamation was issued. It eventually brought about the downfall of slavery. As the Union armies advanced into the South, thousands of slaves fled the plantations. When the war ended with victory for the Union, former slaves, now called freedmen, joyfully embraced freedom.

Letters from slaves
These letters, written after the abolition of slavery, give a clear picture of how slaves felt about being free.

The defeated southern states were brought back into the Union through a process called **Reconstruction.** To reenter the Union, white southerners had to give their former slaves new rights. Three amendments (changes or additions)—the Thirteenth, Fourteenth, and Fifteenth—were added to the **Constitution.** They abolished slavery and gave the freedmen the right to vote and the protection of the law.

To the fury of the white southerners, Union soldiers carrying rifles and bayonets were stationed throughout the South to guarantee the freedmen's rights. In 1877, the Union soldiers were pulled out of the South. Southern whites regained control, and they had no intention of treating their former slaves as equals.

Robert Purvis, a former slave, wrote about the changes in the United States during the Civil War.

This photograph, taken during the Civil War, shows escaped slaves on a plantation that had been captured by Union soldiers. These escaped slaves never returned to their former owners.

Dear Mrs. Cheney,

I felt I would like to write to you a line from my old home. I am sitting under the old roof twelve feet from the spot where I suffered all the crushing weight of slavery. Thank God the bitter cup is drained of its last dreg. There is no need for more hiding places.

I cannot tell you how I feel in this place. The change is so great I can hardly take it all in. I was born here . . . I have hunted up all the old people, done what I could for them . . . many of them I have known since childhood.

I never saw such a state of excitement . . .

Hi Jacobs

Sir, old things are passing away, all things are becoming new. Now a black man has rights, under this government, which every white man, here and everywhere, is bound to respect. . . . The slave power no longer rules in Washington. The slaveholders and their miserable allies are biting the dust.

Jim Crow

With the **Union** troops gone, white southerners moved quickly to return African Americans to a state of near slavery. They created a set of laws, called **Jim Crow** laws, which took away the rights African Americans had recently been guaranteed in the **Constitution.** These laws kept African Americans from owning property, taking well-paid jobs, or testifying in court against a white person. From the late 1880s to the early 1900s, the South turned itself into a society where African Americans and whites were kept apart by a system of **segregation.**

No part of southern life was left untouched by Jim Crow. All public places in the South were divided by race: public bathrooms, trains, courts, theaters, schools, buses, and even parks and swimming areas. Southern whites insisted that segregation was fair. They said the races were separate but equal. In reality, however, this was rarely true. For example, even though both African Americans and whites paid taxes, the schools that white children attended received more tax money.

Those who challenged Jim Crow were often denied jobs as well as loans from local banks. Others were arrested, beaten, or killed. Groups like the **Ku Klux Klan** used murder and violence to bully African Americans into submission. Still, African Americans battled against Jim Crow. They insisted that separating the races was breaking the law. In 1896, the **Supreme Court** issued a crushing decision known as *Plessy v. Ferguson,* which supported Jim Crow.

The Ku Klux Klan, shown here marching through a southern town in 1925, has been guilty of using violence and murder in support of its beliefs that white people are superior to all people of color and that the races should be strictly segregated.

John Marshall Harlan angrily disagrees with Supreme Court ruling

Supreme Court Justice John Marshall Harlan disagreed with the *Plessy v. Ferguson* ruling of 1896, which said separating the races was legal as long as conditions were equal.

The white race deems itself to be the dominant race in this country. But in the view of the Constitution, in the eye of the law, there is in this country no superior, dominant ruling class of citizens. Our Constitution is color-blind. In respect of civil rights, all citizens are equal before the law. It is, therefore, to be regretted that [the Supreme Court] has reached the conclusion to regulate civil rights solely upon the basis of race.

We boast of the freedom enjoyed by our people above all other peoples. But it is difficult to reconcile that boast with a law which, practically, puts the brand of servitude [near slavery] and degradation [humiliation] upon a large class of our fellow citizens. The thin disguise of "equal" accommodations will not mislead anyone, nor atone [make up] for the wrong this day done.

Supreme Court Justice John Marshall Harlan was disgusted when the Supreme Court upheld segregation in an 1896 decision. He believed that all U.S. citizens should be equal before the law.

15

Calls for Equal Rights

Racism and **segregation** were not limited to the South. African Americans faced **discrimination** across the country. Schools were segregated throughout the South as well as in many states in the North and West. African Americans were routinely shut out of well-paid jobs and leadership positions.

During the late 1800s and into the 1900s, hundreds of African-American individuals and organizations battled racism and discrimination. Many African-American leaders, such as Mary McLeod Bethune and Booker T. Washington, believed that education would overcome racism. W. E. B. DuBois, a writer and **activist,** helped found the National Association for the Advancement of Colored People (NAACP) in 1909 to "promote **equality** of rights and eradicate [remove] race prejudice among the citizens of the United States." Supported by both African-American and white activists, the organization battled against laws that kept African Americans out of good housing, schools, and jobs.

But African Americans who served in segregated units during World War I (1914–1918) returned from the war to find that little had changed at home. They still had to eat in separate parts of restaurants and drink from separate water fountains.

The National Association for the Advancement of Colored People was one of the most important organizations to battle racism in the United States. In this photo from the 1930s, a youth council from the association urges others to join their cause.

Ralph Abernathy, who later worked with Martin Luther King Jr., gives an account of what life was like for African Americans living in the segregated southern states.

Blacks were permitted to hold only the menial [humble] jobs, domestic workers and common and ordinary laborers. The only professional jobs that were open to blacks were . . . pastoring a black church and the school teaching profession, which was open because of segregated schools. White teachers didn't normally teach black students. In the whole state of Alabama we had probably less than five black doctors. And we didn't do anything but dig ditches and work with some white supervisor that told us everything to do. We were the last to be hired and the first to be fired.

All of the restaurants were segregated, the hotels and motels were segregated. Meaning that black people were not permitted to live in these hotels. Even in the public courthouse, blacks could not drink water except from the fountain labeled "Colored." You could not use a filling [gas] station that was not designated with a restroom for colored. You had a restroom for white males and a restroom for white women, and you had a restroom for colored. Meaning that colored people had to use the same restroom, male and female. And the janitor never would clean up the restroom for the colored people.

Brown v. Board of Education of Topeka

The NAACP decided to use the law to fight **segregation.** In the 1930s, NAACP lawyers brought cases to court to show that segregated schools were unequal and crippled the education of African-American students. Students also took matters into their own hands. In April 1951, 450 African-American students at Moton High School in Farmville, Virginia, walked out of their school. They protested because their school had no cafeteria and no gym, and because it was crowded with twice as many students as the building could safely hold. Also, Moton High School teachers were paid far less than the white teachers who taught at the local white high school.

The issues raised by the Moton High School students applied to hundreds of other schools. The NAACP, through a group called the Legal Defense Fund, filed more and more lawsuits. One case was brought against the Board of Education in Topeka, Kansas. Oliver Brown, an African-American resident, was angry that his seven-year-old daughter had to travel across town to attend school. Another school was much closer, but it was for white students only.

By 1952, Brown's case and several others were being heard by the **Supreme Court.** Standing before the court in Washington, D.C., the NAACP lawyers argued that separating African-American students made them feel inferior. "Separate but equal," they argued, was not possible. On May 17, 1954, the Supreme Court announced its decision in the *Brown v. Board of Education of Topeka* case. Stunning the nation, the justices wrote that segregation did **discriminate** against African-American students. Segregation in schools, the court ruled, was against the law. The victory launched the Civil Rights movement.

Earl Warren announces Supreme Court's decision
Earl Warren, a Supreme Court justice, read the ruling on the *Brown v. Board of Education of Topeka* case which overturned the idea of "separate but equal" in education.

This is a segregated school in Uno, Virginia, in 1947. African-American students went to separate schools and were taught by African-American teachers. White students attended their own schools, which were better funded and had better facilities.

Does segregation of children in public schools solely on the basis of race deprive children of the minority group of equal educational opportunities? We believe it does. To separate them from others of similar age and qualifications solely because of their race generates a feeling of inferiority as to their status in the community that may affect their hearts and minds in a way very unlikely to be undone. We conclude unanimously, that in the field of public education the doctrine of "separate but equal" has no place. Separate educational facilities are inherently [by their nature] unequal.

19

Rosa Parks

The **Supreme Court's** decision was just a beginning. **Segregation** in schools was declared illegal, but segregation still existed almost everywhere else, from theaters to swimming pools.

On buses throughout the South, white people sat in the front and African Americans sat in the back. If the back section filled up, African-American riders could not sit in the white section even if seats were available. If the bus was crowded, they were forced to give their seats to whites. On December 1, 1955, a 43-year-old African-American woman named Rosa Parks boarded a bus in Montgomery, Alabama. Exhausted after a long day, Parks sat down. The bus continued on its route and filled up with passengers. When a white man boarded, the bus driver turned and ordered Parks to give up her seat. She refused and was arrested. Her simple act of defiance inspired an entire city and later an entire country.

Montgomery's African-American community was outraged that Parks, a quiet, hardworking woman, had been arrested. Many African-American groups and ministers who had looked to challenge bus segregation now decided to take a stand. They selected a leader, a 26-year-old minister named Martin Luther King Jr.

This map shows the states that formed the Confederacy during the **Civil War** and that are today referred to as the South.

Key
Present-day states that made up the Confederate States of America during the Civil War (1861–1865)

CANADA

UNITED STATES OF AMERICA

Boston

Chicago

New York City

Washington, D.C.

VIRGINIA

Greensboro
Raleigh

TENNESSEE   N. CAROLINA

ARKANSAS Memphis   S. CAROLINA
           Birmingham   Atlanta
Little Rock   MISSISSIPPI
           Selma Montgomery
TEXAS   Jackson ALABAMA Albany
           LOUISIANA   GEORGIA
           New Orleans   St. Augustine
                          FLORIDA

MEXICO

0   800 km
0   500 miles

N
W —— E
S

Rosa Parks's account

In an interview given some years after the event, Rosa Parks recalls the moment when she refused to give up her bus seat.

This one man was standing and when the driver looked around and saw he was standing he asked the four of us, the man in the seat with me and the two women across the aisle, to let him have those front seats. At his first request, didn't any of us move. Then he spoke again and said "You'd better make it light on yourselves and let me have those seats." . . . When the three people stood up and moved into the aisle, I remained where I was. When the driver saw that I was still sitting there, he asked if I was going to stand up. I told him, no, I wasn't. He said, "Well, if you don't stand up, I'm going to have you arrested." I told him to go on and have me arrested.

The Montgomery Bus Boycott

Martin Luther King Jr. and other African-American leaders decided to launch a **boycott** of Montgomery's buses. The boycott was organized by the Montgomery Improvement Association (MIA). By refusing to ride the buses, the boycotters hoped the bus companies would lose money and be forced to abandon their **segregation** policy.

Montgomery's white leaders laughed at the idea of the boycott, predicting that it would quickly fail. After all, many of Montgomery's African-American residents relied on the buses to get to and from work, to shop, and to visit friends.

On December 5, 1955, the first day of the boycott, the buses pulled up to normally packed stops. This time there were few riders. The buses continued on, their seats empty. African-American taxi drivers and residents with cars began a car pool to carry riders where they needed to go. Others simply walked. Montgomery's white leaders were angry and confused, but they refused to give in. In February 1956, angry whites bombed several African-American leaders' homes. Martin Luther King Jr. was arrested and jailed.

But inspired by King's leadership and speeches, Montgomery's African-American community held firm. In November 1956, the **Supreme Court** ruled that segregation on buses was illegal. After more than a year, African-American residents boarded the buses again, free to sit wherever they wished. After the success of the boycott, an organization called the Southern Christian Leadership Conference (SCLC) was formed to coordinate more protests. King was elected as its first president.

Virginia Durr describes her feelings
Not all whites were against the boycott. Virginia Durr, a white woman who lived in Montgomery at that time, believed that a great injustice had been removed.

Martin Luther King Jr., shown here seated on the left and wearing a hat, was chosen to be the leader of the Montgomery Improvement Association, the organization that protested against segregation on city buses. King's leadership and the success of the boycott catapulted him onto the national stage and made him one of the greatest leaders of the civil rights era.

Jo Ann Robinson describes her feelings

After the success of the boycott, many African Americans felt that they had a new power to force change in America. **Activist** Jo Ann Robinson described this feeling of power and joy.

We felt that we were somebody. That somebody has listened to us, that we had forced the white man to give what we knew was our own citizenship. And if you have never had the feeling that you are no longer an alien, but that this is your country too, then you don't know what I am talking about. It is a hilarious feeling that just goes all over you, that makes you feel that America is a great country and we're going to do more to make it greater.

When I heard that the boycott had been successful, I felt pure, unadulterated [absolute] joy. It was like a fountain of joy. Of course the blacks felt that way, but the white friends I had felt the way I did. We felt joy and release. It was as if a great burden had fallen off us.

23

Showdown at Little Rock

Despite the *Brown v. Board of Education* decision, **segregated** schools continued to exist. In Little Rock, the capital of Arkansas, mothers of white students fiercely protested the proposed **desegregation** of the high school in 1957. Arkansas governor Orval Faubus stepped in.

When the school year began, Faubus called in the National Guard to surround the school, barring African-American students. He claimed he was taking this action for fear of armed **racist** groups. On September 4, nine African-American students went to the school. A mob of local people threatened them, and the soldiers turned them away. Two weeks later, the NAACP succeeded in a legal action to stop Faubus from using the National Guard this way. On September 23, the students were taken into the school through a side door. The rage outside was so great that by mid-morning they had to leave. Infuriated, President Dwight Eisenhower sent **federal** troops to act as personal guards for the "Little Rock Nine." On September 24, they started school, taken to and from class by armed soldiers.

Elizabeth Eckford, one of the "Little Rock Nine," tries to ignore the taunts that come from a crowd of whites as she walks to the entrance of Little Rock High School on September 4, 1957. She was not allowed to enter the school that day.

These federal troops, ordered to Little Rock by President Eisenhower, surround Little Rock High School to make sure that African-American students can safely attend class. The soldiers picked up the students at the beginning of the school day, took them to their classes, and drove them home in the afternoon.

Elizabeth Eckford's account

Elizabeth Eckford, one of the original nine Little Rock students, spoke about the first terrifying moments when she arrived alone at the school.

All I could hear was the shuffling of their feet. Then someone shouted, "Here she comes, get ready!" The crowd moved in closer and then began to follow me, calling me names. I still wasn't afraid. Just a little bit nervous. Then my knees started to shake all of a sudden and I wondered whether I could make the center entrance a block away. It was the longest block I ever walked in my whole life. I walked until I was right in front of the path to the front door. I stood looking at the school—it looked so big! Just then the guards let some white students through. The crowd was quiet. I guess they were waiting to see what was going to happen. When I was able to steady my knees, I walked up to the guard who had let the white students in. He too didn't move. When I tried to squeeze past him, he raised his bayonet and then the other guards moved in and they raised their bayonets. They glared at me with a mean look and I was very frightened and didn't know what to do.

Nonviolent Resistance

Protests against **segregation** broke out in cities across the United States. Most of these early protests were **nonviolent.** By remaining nonviolent, the demonstrators hoped to show the justice of their cause and change the minds of those who resisted change. Many civil rights leaders had been influenced by Mohandas Gandhi, whose peaceful demonstrations had helped bring about India's independence from British rule in 1947.

Sit-ins are an example of nonviolent resistance. In the mid-1900s, restaurants in many parts of the country still seated African Americans and whites in separate sections. Groups of African-American students broke down segregation by sitting in the white section of restaurants and ordering food. When they were refused, as usually happened, they would not leave. They simply sat there, expressing their protest by sitting. The first sit-in occurred in Greensboro, North Carolina, in 1960.

Although sit-ins were nonviolent, the reaction to them often was not. Students were cursed at, pelted with food, and sometimes beaten. Often they were arrested and jailed by police for disturbing the peace. The sit-in participants were taught not to respond to taunts. They were told to shield themselves and stay in their seats.

Sit-ins spread to cities around the country, and thousands of students participated. In 1960, students who participated in sit-ins formed the Student Nonviolent Coordinating Committee (SNCC).

In May 1963, these students hold a sit-in protest at a lunch counter in Jackson, Mississippi. One of the protesters has been covered in sugar and ketchup thrown by people in the crowd.

We went over to the counter and asked to be served coffee and doughnuts. As anticipated, the reply was, "I'm sorry we don't serve you here." The attendant or waitress was a little bit dumbfounded. At that point there was a policeman who had walked in off the street, who was pacing the aisle behind us, where we were seated, with his club in his hand, just sort of knocking it in his hand, and just looking mean and red and little bit upset and little bit disgusted. And you had the feeling that for the first time this big bad man with the gun and the club has been pushed in a corner and he's got absolutely no defense, and the thing that's killing him more than anything else—he doesn't know what he can or what he cannot do. He's defenseless. Usually his defense is offense, and we've provoked him, yes, but we haven't provoked him outwardly enough for him to resort to violence. And I think this is just killing him; you can see it all over him.

Freedom Rides

The battle against **segregation** was taken to the nation's interstate bus system. The **Supreme Court** had ruled that segregation on buses that traveled across state lines was against the law, yet segregation still existed. When buses crossed from northern states into southern states, African-American and white passengers had to move to separate sections. Also, when the buses stopped at stations in the South, passengers still faced segregated bathrooms, waiting areas, and drinking fountains.

In the spring of 1961, a group of people from the Congress of Racial **Equality** (CORE) decided to **desegregate** the nation's long-distance bus service. On May 4, 1961, thirteen white and African-American CORE members boarded a bus in Washington, D.C. They called themselves Freedom Riders and they refused to sit according to race.

The Freedom Riders were not welcome. In Anniston, Alabama, an angry crowd pelted the bus with stones and slashed the tires. When the bus raced out of the town and stopped for the tires to be changed, the mob followed and threw a fire bomb into the front door. The riders escaped as the bus burned. Despite the violence, the Freedom Rides continued. More riders followed, and many were attacked and beaten. Others were jailed. After the long summer of 1961, however, segregation on the nation's interstate buses could not continue. It came to an end in September 1961 after a ruling from the **Interstate Commerce Commission.**

This photograph captures the moments after a white mob caught up with a bus carrying Freedom Riders into the South. The bus boils with smoke and flames. Freedom Riders sit in the foreground.

28

Jim Zwerg speaks to reporters

On May 20, 1961, Jim Zwerg, a white Freedom Rider, was beaten in Montgomery, Alabama, by a group of whites. Lying in a hospital bed and covered with cuts and bruises, he spoke to a reporter.

Segregation must be stopped. It must be broken down. Those of us who are on the Freedom Rides will continue. I'm not sure if I'll be able to, but we are going on to New Orleans no matter what happens. We are dedicated to this. We will take hitting. We'll take beatings. We're willing to accept death. But we are going to keep coming until we can ride from anywhere in the South to anyplace else in the South, as Americans, without anyone making any comment.

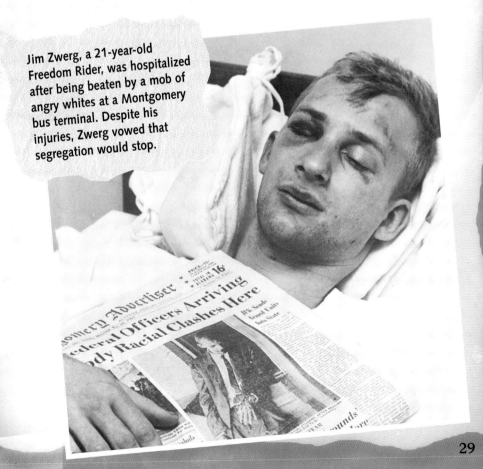

Jim Zwerg, a 21-year-old Freedom Rider, was hospitalized after being beaten by a mob of angry whites at a Montgomery bus terminal. Despite his injuries, Zwerg vowed that segregation would stop.

29

The Battle of Birmingham

Martin Luther King Jr. called Birmingham, Alabama, "probably the most thoroughly **segregated** city in the United States." In 1963, almost every facility, from buses to theaters to drinking fountains, separated the 350,000 African-American and white residents. Declaring that "as Birmingham goes, so goes the South," King was determined to shatter segregation in the city.

In the spring of 1963, King began organizing protests and the **picketing** of city businesses. The Southern Christian Leadership Conference (SCLC) produced a list of demands that, if followed, would bring about **desegregation.** King was arrested and sent to jail. In a newspaper article, a group of Birmingham business, religious, and **civic** leaders called King a troublemaker and urged him to stop demonstrating against segregation. Instead, they said, King should be more patient and wait for change.

King, alone in his jail cell, wrote a letter in response to this argument. The document, "Letter from a Birmingham Jail," has become a classic piece of writing from the Civil Rights movement.

Birmingham **activists** discuss the different tactics needed to break segregation. Shops that were segregated were targeted by **boycotts.** In this photograph, a demonstrator holds up a sign that will later be used in the demonstration. It reads, "Why Buy Segregation"?

Martin Luther King Jr. writes from jail

Here is an excerpt from King's letter explaining why African Americans were no longer content to wait for civil rights.

For years now I have heard the word "Wait!" It rings in the ear of every Negro [African American] with piercing familiarity. This "Wait" has always meant "Never." We have waited more than 340 years for our constitutional and God-given rights. Perhaps it is easy for those who have never felt the stinging darts of segregation to say, "Wait." But . . . when you suddenly find your tongue twisted and your speech stammering as you seek to explain to your six-year-old daughter why she can't go to the public amusement park that has just been advertised on television, and see tears welling up in her eyes when she is told that Funtown is closed to colored children, and see ominous clouds of inferiority beginning to form in her little mental sky, and see her beginning to distort [twist] her personality by developing an unconscious bitterness toward white people; when you take a cross-country drive and find it necessary to sleep night after night in the uncomfortable corners of your automobile because no motel will accept you; when you are humiliated day in and day out by nagging signs reading "white" and "colored"; when you are fighting a degenerating [gradually worsening] sense of "nobodiness"—then you will understand why we find it so difficult to wait.

Martin Luther King Jr. was often arrested and taken to jail. King used his own imprisonment to draw attention to his cause. He also wrote persuasive defenses of his tactics, such as the classic "Letter from a Birmingham Jail."

The Children's March

With King in jail, the protests in Birmingham began to collapse. Sensing a crisis, civil rights leaders in Birmingham decided on a new strategy. A group of African-American children would march in Birmingham to protest against **racism.** If the children of Birmingham couldn't awaken America's conscience, they thought, then nothing would.

On May 2, 1963, the children, aged six and over, marched, singing and clapping. Almost 1,000 children were arrested and taken to jail. The next day, the city's commissioner of public safety, Bull Connor, ordered the city's firemen to direct powerful hoses at the remaining children. The jets of water blasted them against buildings and knocked them down streets. Shocked and enraged, Birmingham's African-American community showed up by the thousands the next day. This time the demonstrators were met by growling attack dogs as well as fire hoses.

The photographs of demonstrators huddling along walls and by trees were seen in newspapers and on televisions around the world. Feelings of disgust and rage from across the nation and around the world descended on Birmingham. President John F. Kennedy had sympathized with the civil rights cause, but had not wanted to upset white southern voters. After Birmingham, however, he realized something had to be done.

Three civil rights demonstrators cling to each other as they are blasted with water from fire hoses. Images like this photo, taken during the protests in Birmingham in May 1963, were shown on television screens and in newspapers around the world.

President John F. Kennedy's speech

A few weeks after the children's march, on June 11, 1963, President Kennedy delivered a national speech that promised to introduce new **legislation** in support of civil rights.

The heart of the question is whether all Americans are to be afforded equal rights and equal opportunities; whether we are going to treat our fellow Americans as we want to be treated.

If an American, because his skin is dark, cannot eat lunch in a restaurant open to the public; if he cannot send his children to the best public schools available; if he cannot vote for the public officials who represent him; if, in short, he cannot enjoy the full and free life, which all of us want, then who among us would be content to have the color of his skin changed and stand in his place?

Who among us would then be content with the counsels of patience and delay? One hundred years of delay have passed since President Lincoln freed the slaves, yet their heirs, their grandsons, are not fully free. . . .

And this nation, for all its hopes and all its boasts, will not be fully free until all its citizens are free. Now the time has come for the nation to fulfill its promise.

President John F. Kennedy, like President Eisenhower before him, was at first reluctant to involve the national government in the civil rights controversy. However, the violence that surrounded the demonstrations in Birmingham forced him to call for new civil rights legislation.

March on Washington

With the confrontation in Birmingham still smoldering, President Kennedy introduced **legislation** into **Congress** to abolish **segregation** in public places and **discrimination** in the job market. As the legislation was being debated in the halls of Congress, African-American leaders decided to organize a mass demonstration in the nation's capital. The March on Washington would show the nation and its leaders the vital importance of civil rights. The leaders called for the march to take place at the end of August 1963.

News of the march spread and thousands of African-American and white supporters planned to attend. Dozens of trains and more than 2,000 buses were used to transport marchers from different parts of the country. On August 28, more than 250,000 demonstrators filled the National Mall in front of the Lincoln Memorial in Washington, D.C.

Dozens of speakers gave speeches at a podium set before the statue of Abraham Lincoln. Many remarked that it had been 100 years since the Emancipation Proclamation was signed, which eventually ended slavery in the South.

At the end of the day, Martin Luther King Jr. gave his now famous "I Have a Dream" speech. In it, he described his hope that the U.S. would become a nation that honored the rights of all of its citizens, regardless of their skin color.

King stands before a crowd of hundreds of thousands in Washington, D.C., and delivers his "I Have a Dream" speech. He called for a color-blind society built on trust and love. The speech has become a classic statement of the Civil Rights movement.

Martin Luther King's "I Have a Dream" speech
Of all of the speeches given on that day, King's speech, with its repetition of the phrase "I have a dream," was the one that everyone would remember.

So I say to you, my friends, that even though we must face the difficulties of today and tomorrow, I still have a dream. It is a dream deeply rooted in the American dream that one day this nation will rise up and live out the true meaning of its creed — "We hold these truths to be self evident that all men are created equal."

I have a dream that one day on the red hills of Georgia, sons of former slaves and sons of former slave owners will be able to sit down together at the table of brotherhood.

I have a dream that one day, even the state of Mississippi, a state sweltering with the heat of oppression, will be transformed into an oasis of freedom and justice.

I have a dream that my four little children will one day live in a nation where they will not be judged by the color of their skin, but by the content of their character. I have a dream today!

Freedom Summer

In 1964, **activists** launched a bold campaign to end **segregation** in Mississippi, a state in the heartland of the South. Civil rights leaders invited African-American and white students from around the country to come to Mississippi. In a project called Freedom Summer, hundreds of students, mostly from the northeast, answered the call. The students spread out into the Mississippi countryside, trying to register African Americans to vote. In the 1950s, only 5 percent of voting-age African Americans were registered to vote. Many more wanted to register, but worried that if they did they might lose their jobs. With the power to vote, the civil-rights activists hoped that African-American Mississippians could influence political decision-making in their state.

White Mississippians regarded the Freedom Summer project as a hostile invasion by outsiders. Allen Thompson, the mayor of Jackson, Mississippi, expanded the police force, purchased 250 shotguns, and planned to use the nearby fairgrounds as a prison.

Freedom Summer was filled with violence. Some civil rights workers were shot at and **harassed.** Three workers, two white and one African American, were murdered. Many more were arrested. The summer also changed the attitudes and outlook of thousands of African-American Mississippians. For many, especially those who lived in the countryside, it was the first time they had heard such a message of hope.

THE FBI IS SEEKING INFORMATION CONCERNING THE DISAPPEARANCE AT PHILADELPHIA, MISSISSIPPI, OF THESE THREE INDIVIDUALS ON JUNE 21, 1964. EXTENSIVE INVESTIGATION IS BEING CONDUCTED TO LOCATE GOODMAN, CHANEY, AND SCHWERNER, WHO ARE DESCRIBED AS FOLLOWS:

	ANDREW GOODMAN	JAMES EARL CHANEY	MICHAEL HENRY SCHWERNER
RACE:	White	Negro	White
SEX:	Male	Male	Male
DOB:	November 23, 1943	May 30, 1943	November 6, 1939
POB:	New York City	Meridian, Mississippi	New York City
AGE:	20 years	21 years	24 years
HEIGHT:	5'10"	5'7"	5'9" to 5'10"
WEIGHT:	150 pounds	135 to 140 pounds	170 to 180 pounds
HAIR:	Dark brown; wavy	Black	Brown
EYES:	Brown	Brown	Light blue
TEETH:		Good; none missing	
SCARS AND MARKS:		1 inch cut scar 2 inches above left ear.	Pock mark center of forehead, slight scar on bridge of nose, appendectomy scar, broken leg scar.

SHOULD YOU HAVE OR IN THE FUTURE RECEIVE ANY INFORMATION CONCERNING THE WHEREABOUTS OF THESE INDIVIDUALS, YOU ARE REQUESTED TO NOTIFY ME OR THE NEAREST OFFICE OF THE FBI. TELEPHONE NUMBER IS LISTED BELOW.

Three young civil rights workers, Andrew Goodman, James Earl Chaney, and Michael Henry Schwerner, disappeared in Mississippi during June 1964. Their bodies were later found buried in a dam. A **federal** investigation discovered that members of the **Ku Klux Klan** were responsible for the murders.

Fannie Lou Hamer's account

Freedom Summer directly affected the attitudes of thousands of African-American Mississippians. Here, Fannie Lou Hamer describes how a Freedom Summer volunteer changed her life.

Until then I'd never heard of no mass meeting and I didn't know that a Negro (African American) could register and vote. Bob Moses, Reffie Robinson, Jim Bevel, and James Forman were some of the SNCC [Student Nonviolent Coordinating Committee] workers who ran that meeting. When they asked for those to raise their hands who'd go down to the courthouse the next day, I raised mine. Had it up as high as I could get it. I guess if I'd had any sense I'da been a little scared, but what was the point of being scared? The only thing they could do to me was kill me and it seemed like they'd been trying to do that a little bit at a time ever since I could remember.

William Simmons's account

Many white Mississippians were infuriated by the Freedom Summer volunteers. William Simmons, spokesman for the White Citizens' Council, an organization that openly worked to preserve segregation, tells how the volunteers angered a lot of people.

They were met with a feeling of some curiosity, but mostly resentment [displeasure]. They fanned out across the state, made a great to-do of breaking up our customs, of flouting [scoffing at] social practices that had been respected by people here over the years. The arrogance they showed in wanting to reform the whole state created resentment. So to say they were not warmly received and welcomed is perhaps an understatement.

The Civil Rights Act

As Freedom Summer was launched in Mississippi, members of **Congress** in Washington, D.C., debated a new civil rights bill. President Kennedy, who was **assassinated** in November 1963, had failed to get any important civil rights laws passed. The new president, Lyndon B. Johnson from Texas, pledged his support for the new bill. The bill faced opposition in Congress, where many white lawmakers from the South were determined to vote against it. After long and bitter debates, however, the bill was passed. Johnson signed it into law on July 2, 1964. The act was the most important set of laws passed for civil rights since **Reconstruction.** Finally, the South's **Jim Crow** laws would be dismantled.

The act made **discrimination** and **segregation** illegal and gave the **federal** government special powers to combat racial discrimination in education and employment. For many white supporters of the Civil Rights movement, the Civil Rights Act was the final victory after a long period of protest and unrest. But for African Americans, the Civil Rights Act of 1964 was just the beginning.

President Lyndon B. Johnson, surrounded by dozens of supporters and journalists, signs the Civil Rights Act into law in 1964.

President Lyndon B. Johnson's speech

President Kennedy had submitted the Civil Rights Bill to Congress, but his assassination prevented him from turning the bill into law. It was his successor, President Lyndon B. Johnson, a southerner, who signed the Civil Rights Act into law on July 2, 1964. Here is an excerpt from the speech that he gave on this momentous occasion.

Americans of every race and color have died in battle to protect our freedom. Americans of every race and color have worked to build a nation of widening opportunities. Now our generation of Americans has been called on to continue the unending search for justice within our own borders.

We believe that all men are created equal. Yet many are denied equal treatment.

We believe that all men have certain unalienable rights. Yet many Americans do not enjoy those rights.

We believe that all men are entitled to the blessings of liberty. Yet millions are being deprived of those blessings — not because of their own failures, but because of the color of their skin.

The reasons are deeply imbedded in history and tradition and the nature of man. We can understand — without rancor [ill will] or hatred — how this all happened.

But it cannot continue. Our Constitution, the foundation of our Republic, forbids it. The principles of our freedom forbid it. Morality forbids it. And the law I will sign tonight forbids it.

Slow to Change

The Civil Rights Act was a great victory, but it caused a huge backlash. Many white Americans were still not ready to treat African Americans as equals. In the South, the **Ku Klux Klan** continued to use violence against people who challenged **segregation.** Other groups, called White Citizens' Councils, worked to preserve segregation, defending it as their "way of life." White candidates for office said they would never let the walls of segregation fall. Many of those candidates were voted into office with overwhelming support.

Civil rights **activists** tried to register African Americans to vote. But those who did register faced **harassment.** When they showed up to vote, they were quizzed about American history or asked to explain parts of the **Constitution.** If they answered incorrectly, they were not allowed to vote. Others were charged a tax in order to vote that they could not afford. Whites rarely faced such hurdles.

The first demonstrators who tried to march from Selma to Montgomery were stopped by state police. In a few terrifying moments, state police attacked the demonstrators with tear gas and clubs. This woman collapsed after being overwhelmed by tear gas.

As a result, few African Americans voted. In Selma, Alabama, for example, only 156 of the city's 15,000 eligible African-American residents were registered to vote. In March 1965, King led protests in Selma. After violent clashes with the police, he announced he would lead a 54-mile (86-kilometer) march through Alabama to the state capital, Montgomery. The march put pressure on lawmakers. In 1965, **Congress** passed the Voting Rights Act. It removed most of the barriers that prevented African Americans from registering and voting.

Protest songs

An observer of a civil rights protest could usually count on hearing at least one common element—a song. Many protest songs came from African-American churches. One song, called "We Shall Overcome," has been called the **anthem** of the Civil Rights movement. The words come from a gospel song written by Charles Tindley in 1900.

We shall overcome
We shall overcome
We shall overcome some day
Oh deep in my heart
I do believe
We shall overcome some day.

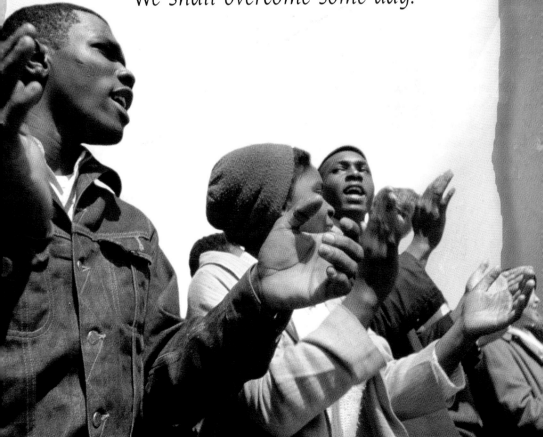

Malcolm X and Black Power

By the mid-1960s, many whites were losing patience with the Civil Rights movement, declaring that it had already achieved its aims. African Americans, in the meantime, were angered by the lack of progress. Despite new laws, African Americans still suffered from a lack of good jobs, schools, and housing.

These problems were worse in the cities, where large populations lived in crowded neighborhoods far from jobs and services. For the African Americans who lived under those conditions, the Civil Rights movement was failing. In 1965, the anger and frustration exploded into riots. The Watts neighborhood of Los Angeles was devastated in six days of burning and looting. Thirty-four people were killed and more than one thousand were injured. In the following years, race riots ravaged dozens of cities.

Some African-American leaders, such as Malcolm X and Stokely Carmichael, supported a new Black Power movement. Their ideas were more violent and aggressive than King's and the students' peace-centered movements. These movements also urged African Americans to take pride in themselves and in the achievements of African-American culture.

The anger of African-Americans at the slow pace of change and poverty in inner cities exploded into riots during the late 1960s. In this photo, police search African-American youths during riots in the Watts area of Los Angeles.

Malcolm X delivers a speech in Harlem in May 1963. Eloquent and passionate, Malcolm X urged African Americans to take greater pride in themselves and their community and to battle against white injustice.

The words of Malcolm X

In his writings and speeches, Malcolm X often criticized the **nonviolent** approach of **activists** such as Martin Luther King Jr. He argued that the use of violence as a means of self-defense was justifiable. After 1964, he began to moderate some of his views. In 1965, he was **assassinated.**

The common goal of 22 million Afro-Americans is respect as human beings, the God-given right to be a human being. Our common goal is to obtain the human rights that America has been denying us. We can never get civil rights in America until our human rights are first restored. We will never be recognized as citizens there until we are first recognized as humans.

I believe in the brotherhood of man, all men, but I don't believe in brotherhood with anybody who doesn't want brotherhood with me. I believe in treating people right, but I'm not going to waste my time trying to treat somebody right who doesn't know how to return the treatment.

Assassinations and Riots

In the late 1960s, the United States experienced more unrest as thousands of American soldiers were fighting and dying in the **Vietnam War.** Supporters of the war said it was necessary to prevent the spread of **communism.** Many Americans openly disagreed and tens of thousands of them protested in the streets.

As the debate over the war raged, Martin Luther King Jr. and other civil rights leaders continued to demonstrate for equal rights. In 1966, King went to Chicago to protest **segregated** housing and the lack of services for the city's African-American residents. When he led demonstrations into areas where whites lived, King was stunned by the angry taunting and resistance of the white crowds.

Through 1967 and 1968, riots and unrest shook cities across the country. On April 4, 1968, King was **assassinated** on his hotel balcony in Memphis, Tennessee. His murder shocked the country, and condolences poured in from around the world.

By the end of the 1960s, the Civil Rights movement had broken into several groups with different goals and different ideas. One group called the Black Panthers urged African Americans to withdraw from white society and use violence, if necessary, to protect themselves.

The assassination of Martin Luther King Jr. robbed the nation of one of its most eloquent and respected defenders of civil rights. Here, at his funeral in Atlanta, thousands follow the simple wagon that carried his coffin to the cemetery.

Elaine Brown describes members of the Black Panther Party

The Black Panther Party—founded in Oakland, California, in 1966—was formed to protect African-Americans from police brutality. Elaine Brown, who became the first woman to lead the Black Panther Party in 1974, describes the party's membership.

The party reached out mostly to men, to young, black urban men who were on the streets, who knew that there were no options somewhere in their lives, who were gang members because that was all you could be in order to find some sense of dignity about yourself. We reached out to these people because we had something for them to do with the rest of their lives. In most cases, they were used to violence, they were used to struggle, they were used to fighting just to keep alive. We offered them the opportunity to make their lives meaningful.

This Black Panther poster from the 1960s shows the signature gesture of Black Power—a raised left fist. The Black Panther movement urged African Americans to look back to their origins in Africa for pride and strength.

45

Civil Rights in the 1970s, 1980s, and 1990s

In the decades after the peak of the Civil Rights movement, African-American leaders continued to fight for **equality.** In some cases, African Americans were in worse situations in the 1970s than they had been in the 1950s. A middle class of African-American professionals developed, but many moved from their communities. The communities that remained often became isolated and disintegrated under the pressures of crime, drugs, and unemployment. **Discrimination** remained very real.

At the same time, African Americans also experienced astonishing success, such as would have been unimaginable in the 1950s and 1960s. Hardly more than 100 African Americans held elected positions when the Voting Rights Act was passed in 1965. In 1989, 7,200 elected positions were held by African Americans—almost 5,000 of them in the South.

Affirmative action made higher education more available to African-American students. African Americans began to occupy positions of power and authority. In 1967, Thurgood Marshall became the first African American to serve on the Supreme Court of the United States. (As a lawyer for the NAACP, Marshall had previously argued and won the *Brown v. Board of Education* case in front of the Supreme Court in 1954.) In the 1970s, Barbara Jordan became a respected member of **Congress.** Colin Powell, an army general, oversaw the Gulf War (1990–1991) and later became Secretary of State. In 2000, Condoleezza Rice was appointed National Security Advisor of the United States.

Decades after the Civil Rights movement, African Americans have begun to occupy positions of power in the United States that would not have been open to them during the 1950s and 1960s. Here, Colin Powell addresses members of the press after being sworn in as Secretary of State.

For me, the whole era of affirmative action was something that I saw as representing hope, as representing encouragement, and as representing a chance that American society was going, at least in some kind of way, for the first time in its history to allow people of color to be in a position where their individual capabilities . . . could flower and blossom in ways that had never been the case over the centuries. Without affirmative action, there is no doubt that I would not have been able to go to Saint Joe's. I worked very hard and I wound up graduating number one in my department, and that's when I wound up with the opportunity to go to Yale Law School. So I went to Yale Law School, feeling that I was part of the crest of a social movement. And that American society was finally opening up in some limited ways to allow people of color and blacks in particular to participate in all aspects of American life. It had never happened before in America. And I felt proud and I still do feel proud to be a part of that process.

The Unfinished Revolution

In the decades since the Civil Rights movement, people's opinions about race and **equality** have certainly changed. Because the United States is largely a nation of **immigrants,** it is vital that the civil rights of all Americans be recognized, whether they were born in the United States, immigrated from another country, or are descendants of the original inhabitants—the Native Americans. Americans used to insist that newcomers join the melting pot, that they merge and **assimilate** with the white majority. Today, the melting pot has become more of a mosaic. Although people naturally tend to live near others of the same racial and ethnic origin, Americans are settling into new, diverse communities more than they have ever done before. The flood of Latino, Caribbean, and Asian immigrants coming into the United States over the past 40 years has changed the country from a black and white nation to one of many colors.

African Americans still suffer from conditions of inequality more than other Americans; but today, many thousands graduate from college and move into high-level positions as doctors, lawyers, and managers of powerful companies.

Impossible in the years before the Civil Rights movement, this African-American teacher is reading a story to a group of children from different racial and ethnic backgrounds.

Declaration from the Black Radical Congress
The Black Radical Congress, a group of African-American political **activists,** met in March 1997 to discuss civil rights. Below is an excerpt from their declaration, stating that much remains to be done before African Americans can achieve equality.

Resistance is in our marrow as Black people, given our history in this place. From the Haitian revolution, to the U.S. **abolitionist** movement against slavery, to the twentieth century movement for civil rights and **empowerment,** we have struggled and died for justice.

We believe that the struggle must continue, and with renewed vigor. Our historical experiences suggest to us . . . what a truly just and democratic society should look like: It should be democratic, not just in myth but in practice, a society in which all people— regardless of color, ethnicity, religion, nationality, national origin, sex, sexual orientation, age, family structure, or mental or physical capability—enjoy full human rights, the fruits of their labor, and the freedom to realize their full human potential.

What Have We Learned from the Civil Rights Movement?

At different times in history, people have risen to challenge their rulers about the way they are forced to live. It is often a tragic story with a tragic ending. As people on both sides grow angry, they pick up spears, swords, or guns to get their way. The conflict becomes bitter and violent. People are wounded and die; homes and cities are destroyed.

The Civil Rights movement, like other movements of its kind, could have ended this way. The movement faced furious opposition. Anyone who took part in the movement, from a single demonstrator to the highest leader, faced possible death. But the Civil Rights movement as a whole did not turn violent. Instead, the movement demanded only what was just—that the United States live up to its own ideals as stated in the Declaration of Independence that all men are created equal.

By using **nonviolent** tactics, the movement confronted **racism** in a way that stirred the conscience of society and changed the hearts as well as the minds of many people. Today—in government, in schools, in places where Americans work and live—the impact of the Civil Rights movement is visible. It demonstrates that people who look different and who hold different beliefs can still come together to be part of the same community.

On the 37th anniversary of King's "I Have a Dream" speech, the African-American community could be pleased with the progress in American race relations, while also acknowledging the work remaining to be done. Here, protesters bring attention to the problem of police brutality and racial profiling, in which people are stopped by police only because of their race.

END RACISM NOW
PEOPLES ORGANIZATION FOR PROGRESS

Barbara Jordan's speech

Barbara Jordan rose from an impoverished childhood in Texas to become a member of the House of Representatives. In 1976, she became the first African-American woman to deliver the keynote, or most important, address at a political convention. In 1994, she was awarded the Presidential Medal of Freedom, the nation's highest civilian honor. Below is part of Jordan's speech to the Democratic Party Convention, held in New York City in July 1976.

In the past it would have been most unusual for any national political party to ask that a Barbara Jordan deliver a keynote address . . . but tonight here I am. And I feel that . . . my presence here is one additional bit of evidence that the American Dream need not forever be deferred.

We are a people in search of our future. We are a people in search of a national community.

We are attempting to fulfill our national purpose; to create and sustain a society in which all of us are equal.

In this election year we must define the common good and begin again to shape a common good and . . . a common future. . . . A spirit of harmony will survive in America only if each of us remembers that we share a common destiny.

Now, I began this speech by commenting to you on the uniqueness of a Barbara Jordan making the keynote address. Well I am going to close my speech by quoting a Republican President and I ask you that as you listen to these words of Abraham Lincoln, you relate them to the concept of national community in which every last one of us participates:

"As I would not be a slave, so I would not be a master. This expresses my idea of Democracy. Whatever differs from this, to the extent of the difference is no Democracy."

Timeline

1619   The first African slaves are unloaded from a Dutch ship at the English colony of Virginia in North America.

1800s   Slavery becomes the basis of social and economic life in the United States. Slaves, freed blacks, and **abolitionists** use various methods to protest against slavery. Slavery is virtually abolished in the northern states by 1860.

1861–1865   The Civil War is fought.

1863   January: President Abraham Lincoln signs the Emancipation Proclamation as the nation fights a bloody **civil war.** The document legally frees slaves throughout the **rebelling** southern states.

1864–1877   **Reconstruction** in the southern states takes place. African Americans receive many rights, but gradually lose them as white southerners retake power.

1896   **Supreme Court** ruling upholds **segregation** in *Plessy v. Ferguson* case.

1909   The National Association for the Advancement of Colored People is founded by African Americans and whites to fight **discrimination** against African Americans.

1954   May: The Supreme Court issues its landmark decision in *Brown v. Board of Education of Topeka*. The decision rules that segregated education is unequal.

1955   December: Rosa Parks is arrested in Montgomery, Alabama, for refusing to give up her bus seat to a white man. African Americans begin **boycotting** public buses in Montgomery to protest segregation. The boycott lasts more than a year and ends on December 20, 1956, when the Supreme Court upholds a decision that segregation on the buses is illegal.

1956   September: Nine African-American students are turned away by state troops at Little Rock High School in Little Rock, Arkansas. President Dwight Eisenhower orders **federal** soldiers to the high school to guard the students as they attend school.

1960   The first sit-in is held in Greensboro, North Carolina. The tactic is soon imitated by several other groups and is used throughout the United States to fight segregation.

1961   May: The first Freedom Riders ride buses through the South to protest segregation on interstate bus travel. The riders face a combination of mob violence and **harassment** by local police.

1963   Spring: Martin Luther King Jr. leads protests in Birmingham, Alabama, against segregation. After he is arrested, King writes the "Letter from a Birmingham Jail." August: King gives his "I Have A Dream" speech at the foot of the Lincoln Memorial in Washington, D.C.

1964   July: President Lyndon B. Johnson signs the wide-ranging Civil Rights Act. Freedom Summer takes place in Mississippi when civil rights **activists** invite thousands of students to come to Mississippi and register African Americans to vote.

1965   March: Martin Luther King Jr. and other civil rights leaders organize protests in Selma, Alabama, against voting restrictions. The protests meet bitter resistance. August: The Watts neighborhood of Los Angeles is torn by riots. Riots continue to shake cities across the country through the rest of the 1960s. The Voting Rights Act is signed into law. The act makes it illegal to deny someone the right to vote because of his or her race or economic class.

1966	The Black Panther Party is founded in Oakland, California.
1968	April: Martin Luther King Jr. is **assassinated** in Memphis, Tennessee.
1970s and 1980s	Fairer admission and **affirmative action** programs increase the number of African Americans at the nation's colleges and universities.
1986	January: Martin Luther King Jr.'s birthday is honored for the first time as a federal holiday. It is observed every year on the third Monday in January.

Sources for Further Research

Downing, David. *Martin Luther King Jr.* Chicago: Heinemann Library, 2002.

Engelbert, Phillis. *Understanding American Civil Rights.* Farmington Hills, Mich.: Gale Group, 1999.

Fireside, Harvey. *The Mississippi Burning: Civil Rights Murder Conspiracy Trial.* Berkeley Heights, N.J.: Enslow Publishers, 2002.

Kallen, Stuart A. *The Civil Rights Movement.* Edina, Minn.: ABDO Publishing Company, 2001.

Tembo, Limbiko, and Rose Venable. *The Civil Rights Movement.* Eden Prairie, Minn.: The Child's World, 2001.

Weber, Michael. *The African-American Civil Rights Movements.* New York: Raintree Publishers, 1998.

Whitelaw, Nancy. *Mr. Civil Rights: The Story of Thurgood Marshall.* Greensboro, N.C.: Morgan Reynolds Incorporated, 2003.

List of Primary Sources

The author and publisher gratefully acknowledge the following publications and websites from which written sources in the book are drawn. In some cases the wording or sentence structure has been simplified to make the material more appropriate for a school readership.

p. 9 Olaudah Equiano: *The Interesting Narrative and Other Writings.* Edited by Vincent Carretta (New York: Penguin, 1995).

p. 11 Henry Bibb: *Slave Testimony,* John W. Blassingame (Baton Rouge: Louisiana State Press, 1977).

p. 13 Robert Purvis: *Slave Testimony,* John W. Blassingame (Baton Rouge: Louisiana State Press, 1977).

p. 15 "We Shall Overcome: Historic Places of the Civil Rights Movement" http//www.cr.nps.gov/nr/travel/civilrights/change.htm

p. 17 Ralph Abernathy: *Voices of Freedom,* Henry Hampton and Steve Fayer (New York: Bantam Books, 1990).

p. 19 Earl Warren: *Eyes on the Prize,* Juan Williams (New York: Penguin Books, 1987).

p. 21 Rosa Parks: *My Soul Is Rested: Movement Days in the Deep South Remembered,* Howell Raines (New York: Putnam, 1977).

p. 23 Jo Ann Robinson and Virginia Durr: *Eyes on the Prize,* Juan Williams (New York: Penguin Books, 1987).

p. 25 Elizabeth Eckford: *The Long Shadow of Little Rock,* Daisy Gates (Fayetteville: University of Arkansas Press, 1987).

p. 27 Franklin McCain: *My Soul Is Rested: Movement Days in the Deep South Remembered,* Howell Raines (New York: Putnam, 1977).

p. 29 Jim Zwerg: *Eyes on the Prize,* Juan Williams (New York: Penguin Books, 1987).

p. 31 Martin Luther King Jr.: "I Have A Dream." *Writings and Speeches that Changed the World.* Edited by James M. Washington (New York: Harper Collins, 1992).

p. 33 PBS, online site for the program *The American Experience: The Presidents* http://www.pbs.org/wgbh/amex/presidents/nf/resource/ken/primdocs/civilrights.html

p. 35 Martin Luther King Jr.: "I Have A Dream." *Writings and Speeches that Changed the World.* Edited by James M. Washington (New York: Harper Collins, 1992).

p. 37 Fannie Lou Hamer: taped interview by Julius Lester and Maria Varela of the SNCC (1967).

p. 37 William Simmons: *Eyes on the Prize,* Juan Williams (New York: Penguin Books, 1987).

p. 39 President Lyndon B. Johnson: Lyndon Baines Johnson Library and Museum: National Archives and Records Administration. http://www.lbjlib.utexas.edu/Johnson/archives.hom/speeches.hom/640702.asp

p. 41 Charles Tyndley: "We Shall Overcome," 1900

p. 43 Malcolm X: http/www.cmgww.com/historic/malcolm/

p. 45 Elaine Brown: *Voices of Freedom,* Hampton, Henry, and Steve Fayer (New York: Bantam Books, 1990).

p. 47 Luke Harris: *Voices of Freedom,* Hampton, Henry, and Steve Fayer (New York: Bantam Books, 1990).

p. 49 Black Radical Congress: *Let Nobody Turn Us Around.* Edited by Manning Marable and Leith Mullings (New York: Rowman & Littlefield, 2000).

p. 51 Barbara Jordan: Democratic Convention Keynote Address: http://www.elf.net/bjordan/keynote.html

Glossary

abolition forcible ending of a law or custom

activist person who works for a certain cause or issue

affirmative action program implemented in the 1960s that tries to improve the employment or educational opportunities for minority groups and women because they have suffered from discrimination

anthem song that becomes a symbol of a movement, government, or organization

artifact object made and used by people that comes from a certain historical period

assassinate to murder a person, especially for political reasons

assimilate to incorporate the social customs and beliefs of another cultural group

bondage condition of being held against one's will

boycott protest organized by people who try to cause change by deliberately not buying or using something

civic relating to a citizen, city, or citizenship

civil disobedience deliberate breaking of a law because it is unfair. The purpose is to bring attention to the law and help overturn it.

civil war war between groups of people from the same country

communism political system in which private ownership is abolished and industries and services are run by the state

Congress government body that makes laws. It consists of the House of Representatives and the Senate.

constitution written set of guiding principles that state how a country is to be governed

desegregation removing the laws that separate people of one race from another

discrimination treating people unfairly because of their differences, such as race or gender

empowerment given authority or power

equality situation in which people all have the same rights and opportunities

federal relating to the national government

harassment being annoyed or tormented repeatedly

immigrant person who leaves one country to settle in another

Interstate Commerce Commission U.S. government agency that was responsible for regulating the services of companies—such as railroads, trucking companies, and bus lines—involved with transportation between states

Jim Crow term used to describe the racially segregated society created by law in the late nineteenth century in the South. The term came from a fictional character who was an elderly slave.

Ku Klux Klan group formed after the Civil War that was determined to keep whites in power and keep African Americans and white Americans separate by using terrorist tactics

legislation group of laws passed for approval to the governing body of a country

migrant worker worker who moves from place to place to do seasonal work

nonviolence refusal to use force when dealing with others, even if they are violent

picketing protesting outside an organization considered responsible for an injustice

plantation large farm that employed hundreds of people

racism discrimination against people solely on the basis of their race

rally public meeting to discuss and bring attention to an issue

rebellion defiance of the existing order or way of doing things, usually with violence

Reconstruction period after the Civil War when the former Confederate states were brought back into the Union

secede withdraw from a union or existing order

secondary source secondhand account of an event

segregation separation of two or more races in public spaces through law and custom

Supreme Court the highest, most powerful court in the United States

unbiased not allowing personal opinion to affect judgement

Union together, all of the states in the United States; also, the army of the Northern states during the Civil War

Vietnam War (1955–1975) war fought between South Vietnam and the United States against the communist government of North Vietnam

Index